Things That Grow In The Dark

A Story in Poems

Amritaa Sethhi

Made with ❤ on the BookLeaf Publishing Platform
www.bookleafpub.in
www.bookleafpub.com

Dedication

To my younger self, who carried parts of me that I didn't realise I needed. And to everyone who is still learning to love themselves, may you overcome the shadows of doubt and claim the light that has always been yours. I hope you find bliss in your quietest times and never forget that you are more than enough just the way you are.

Preface

Things that Grow in the Dark, is a collection of poems that tells a story. This compilation explores the life of a child who grew up too quickly and spent years restricting herself to fit the roles that were assigned to her. It tells how anxiety took shape in her body before she could even articulate it. How being silent became second nature growing up.

Having all the answers is not the goal of ***Things that Grow in the Dark***. It's about deciding to start over. To provide warmth where only cold existed before. To consciously and gracefully transform into the love you were never fully given.

Anyone who still holds the child they were should read this book.

I hope somewhere in these pages, you find yourself.

I hope you feel seen.

And may you always remember:

Your light was never lost—it was only waiting to be held.

Acknowledgements

I would like to thank my family and friends for their constant support. I hope that every reader who picks up this book will find pieces of themselves in its pages. For every day that I had trouble finding the right words, a part of me was learning how to be seen. And finally, I'm grateful to myself—for showing up, for making peace with what was, and for choosing growth.

The Other Side of the Door

On this side of the door,
I am silence.
Tucked away in a corner,
Where the light doesn't reach,
Holding my breath.

Like waves in the ocean,
The voices rise,
On the other side of the door.
Loud and sharp.
Like the sound of glass breaking.

They think I don't know,
But I can hear the words.
I know the storm rumbling outside,
Cause this isn't the first time.

The door however stays shut.
No one comes in.
No one checks,
If I'm okay,
If I'm listening,
If I'm scared,
If I'm breaking,

Pretending to sleep.

I count the seconds passing,
Between the shouts and the roars.
Keeping on wondering,
If the quiet means it's over, or,
Are they just catching their breath?

On this side of the door,
I practise ignorance by disappearing.
On the other side,
They forget to ask or look for me.

Silence Screams

I was never instructed to be silent,
but challenges taught me things more subtly.
A look, a sigh, the way a room becomes silent,
when the truth is spoken too loudly.
I mastered how to keep all of my ache within
covering it with a kind nod or a well-timed laugh.

My voice was softened, rolled up,
and hidden away in corners,
so that no one could hear it—
a secret I hid even from myself.
Silence became second nature to me.
Safe, undetectable, and predictable.

However, quiet is never really silent.
It waits for the dark to express everything
that the light never allows me to utter,
humming through my bones,
and pressing behind my eyes.

On certain nights, I can still hear it—
the sound of every word I didn't to say,
still trying to get out.

What you Don't See

They put in a lot of work—so much so that
they had no time for tenderness.
Late nights, early mornings, hands constantly working,
and hearts constantly elsewhere.

I received meals, clothes, education
and lessons on how to express gratitude,
even if my voice sounded like a whisper in a loud room.
It was enough, I reassured myself.
that when life is difficult, love feels differently.
that love is not as loud as sacrifice.

However, I still wished their gaze would stay.
for unhurried laughing and consolation
that didn't seem like an afterthought.

The guilt resides in my chest like a forbidden secret.
When they offered so much, how could I possibly be
hurt?
However, a need does not go away because it is
inconvenient.
and suffering doesn't ask as to whether it is justified.

The invisible bruises take longer to heal;

they tend to collect in the calm, waiting,
and still learning how to be loved areas.

I now lovingly carry them,
in truth, rather than blame.

As I am aware of how much they care for me.
But I am also aware that I needed more.

Learning to Listen before Learning to Speak

I was aware of their voices before I even realized my
own.
Sadness could change the space, and fury had a scent.

I observed faces that resembled weather maps,
with the set of jaws predicting storms
and the tension in the temples tracked.
I knew when to act like a bandage,
when to shrink, and when to vanish.

Reading a room before entering it was my first language,
interpreting quietly.
I edited myself,
just to avoid making anyone else feel too strongly.

I took on the role of the mirror,
reflecting back what was required.
a gentleness that resembles an apology,
a smile, and silence.

I simply discovered that
if I remained little enough,
peace could be maintained;

no one told me how.

They referred to me as
helpful, lovely, sweet.
incredibly mature for my age.

However, they never questioned
why I always knew how to cheer others up
while losing touch with how I felt.

I'm unlearning now.
attempting to sit in spaces without changing the air.
allowing other people to control their feelings.

I found this fluency never choosing it,
in the quiet places where kindness never spoke first.

Gold Stars Don't Stick Forever

Gold stars, perfect scores,
and the modest kind of excellence.
I turned it in flawlessly,
as if it were my name.

They said, "Nice job," and turned to the next thing.
My only language became achievement.
Not "how are you?" Just "what's next?"
I came to rely solely on flattering remarks,
confusing acceptance for love.

Years went by.
Burnout manifested as stillness,
inexplicable weeping, and a loss of my sense of what I
enjoyed.
Long after the gold stars stopped sticking,
I continued to pursue them.

However, I'm now beginning to ask myself
the questions that no one else has ever asked:
What do you love?
What is considered enough?

Now I stop when I do well.
I take a breath.
"you did that." I think.

Because I deserve to celebrate little moments.
Rather than always chasing after the big ones.

How do I make Friends?

I assumed it would be simple,
like choosing teams during playtime
or sharing a snack, and then all of a sudden
you had someone with whom you laughed forever.

But it wasn't.

Before you arrive, the circles close.
It consists of jokes you don't yet know,
and whispers with backs turned.
Everyone talks about names you don't know
as if they were secrets that you didn't hear the day they
were told.

I've attended multiple schools, colleges and work places.
I've left people who knew me,
knew how I liked my coffee,
and offered me a seat without asking.

And I carry pieces of my former self in my backpack
when I start over,
but nobody notices them.
I didn't know, there were unwritten norms.
Like how loud you can be without being too much

and who you can laugh with.

I asked to play, waved too quickly, smiled too broadly,
and heard "I already have a partner" too frequently.
I assumed it would be easy, but true friendship feels like
a dance
in which everyone has already learnt the moves and I
didn't.

I occasionally sit quietly and observe.
I still try sometimes.
And perhaps someone will wave back first some day.
Perhaps they will also be new—or simply nice.
Together, we will sit as two parts of a whole.

Mirror Mirror

Mirror, mirror on the wall,
Why do I feel so small ?
Behind these eyes, a thousand thoughts.

However, none that appear to rise
Over the weight of the skin and thighs,
I notice flaws, but nobody is in.

I examine myself from the inside out
and follow the path of every doubt.
Why does love seem like a bluff?
Am I too big, too soft, or not nearly enough?
What would make them look? What is it they would see?
Could it be me, a ghost, or a joke?

I pretend that nothing compares
as I hide beneath these hooded gazes.
Silent anxieties and lip gloss smiles,
Where value is measured in leers and likes.
They claim that I am more than what I appear to be,
yet I would know that mirrors too can lie.

However...
I occasionally dream about strength

and of iron will, when everything else is quiet.
An unbowed girl who dared to think that
beauty is more than just skin deep.
That she might eventually unlearn
the hatred she instilled in herself.

Mirror, mirror—worn and cracked,
Quit reflecting on my tears.
Allow me to view the fire, the battle,
and the silent might in a softer light.
Not as a flaw. Not as a disgrace.
Instead, a shape that has a stable spine
is soft, strong, and entirely mine.
Tell them, if they see me,
that this girl was made of fire and no's.

A Phone Call to the Past

I thought the line would sound hazy,
with your voice still caught in the middle
between sorrow and schoolwork.
However, you picked up as if you had been expecting
this moment the entire time.

"Hey,
I understand that you're busy contemplating
what other people prefer.
I am aware that despite the pressure you put onto it,
your chest seems empty.

Now, though, I need you to pay attention.
Listen for you - just once.

Rest is something you don't have to earn.
Keeping the peace doesn't require you to shrink.
Saying, "What about me?" is acceptable.
That isn't self-centred.
That's how you survive.

You're simply done
of trying to please everyone.

And all that anxiety?
It's not a flaw.
It's only your heart's attempt
to foresee the storm
so that nobody else faces the rain.

However, holding the entire sky
is not your responsibility.

It gets softer, I swear.
You get better at breathing deeply.
You start loving yourself
the way you've always wanted to be loved.

You don't realise how well you're doing.
Simply continue to move forward.

And you'll give this number another call one day—
not to make amends for the past,
but to express your gratitude
to the girl who never gave up."

The Letter that was Never Sent

There was a piece of paper I once discovered
next to the vents under my bed.
Although it had no lines, it felt natural—
a space for writing, breathing, and conversing.

The outside world was harsh and noisy,
with sharply slammed doors and words unkempt.
With icy faces and uncertain hearts,
school was simply a different kind of attempt.

My chest felt tight every day,
but I wasn't sure what to say.
It felt like a small, curled, heavy object
had grown quiet in my universe.

I tried writing:
"I am sorry if I spoke too softly,
misplaced my belongings, or frowned away.
I make an effort to laugh,
but sometimes all I manage to do is cry."

I trembled and so did my pencil.
"But why?" I said after crossing it out.

"Why do I feel so out of place,
like I don't have a real, safe space?"

I described gloomy mornings
and sleepless nights spent sobbing in bed.
Of people who would never notice
the silent, frightened side of me.

So I wrote to no one by name,
hoping someone, somewhere would feel the same.
A hand, a voice, a light to lend—
a secret message I would never send.

And even though it remained in my drawer,
unread, invisible, and forgotten forevermore—
It was my first little letter of hope,
that gave me the strength to cope.

I wished that someone, somewhere, understood
that small hearts can break silently too.

The Staring Contest

Every night begins the same,
with blinking at a white ceiling harshly maimed.
It is half past two, according to the clock.
My mind doesn't care. It never stops.

I blinked. It blinks. The moment of the red lights.
My mind starts its steady, steep climb.
What ifs, what was, and what could have been
echoes more loudly than the world within.

The dark turns into a battlefield
where the loudest sound is silence.
Every breath feels out of place,
and every remembering feels like a tight hug.

The past that refuses to sign its consent,
the friends I lost along the way,
and the future I can't quite create
are all things I collect, which were left unsaid.

The shadows do their small tricks,
like phantom hands holding candle wicks.
And every shape I believe I see
simply stares back, mimicking me.

Once more, it's me against the dark—
a match I lose yet continue to defend.
Sleep fails to begin, eyes wide open.
I'm trapped in this staring competition.

The Empty Chair

What brought you here today?
(Quiet.)
She would have been at a loss for words.
Perhaps they would have laughed, or shrugged.
"I'm fine."
Probably because of the way she was always taught,
to not question everything.

Nobody believed she needed help.
Neither did she.
What is the term for an ordinary ache?
When you've never been taught
that whole isn't the same as heavy?

Someone sitting across from her
may have enquired, "When did it start?"
The answer was - always.
So she would have grinned tightly,
as she always did.

She was raised in homes
where being small was safer
than being noticed.
And where staying quiet

was essential for survival.

Where you treat people's wounds
before they even bleed
and call it love.
Nobody ever questioned.
How about you?

If she had gone,
They could have asked her about the anxiety,
the way her chest always tightened over little matters.
The way her body kept notes
that she never intended to write.

And now, how do you feel?
She would have been unaware.
No one taught her the language of feeling.
All she could do was translate herself into what was
required.

Someone who cares.
A supporting actor.
Too quiet a girl to be worried about.

The chair was never occupied by her.
She repeatedly passed the thought and promised herself
that she would think about it later. Probably.

I'm just exhausted, she told herself.
Nothing at all, she told herself.

The chair, however, does remember.
It bears the burden of what was lost:
the unasked questions, the cries she gulped,
and the woman she could have been
if someone had told her,
"You shouldn't have had to carry all that."
Had she believed them.

Rather, she carried it like a second spine
throughout maturity.
Resilient. Inconspicuous. Invisible.

This is the meeting that never took place.
She didn't ever go inside this particular room.
The girl who needed help,
but didn't believe she ought to receive it
is the subject of this tale.

Monologue

I'm all right. I suppose.
I mean, I ought to be.

Nothing is wrong...
But there's something amiss.
It's all muted.
Heavy and dull.
Like breathing just enough
to stay alive underwater.

Get Up. Brush your teeth.
Smile. Say hello.
Laugh at the joke.
Don't remember what it was about.
Forget what you are about.

Eat something. Scroll.
Disregard the pain.
Disregard the mess that collects
in your chest, the floor, and the desk.

Why am I Tired?
When nothing is all I've done.

What makes quiet seem louder than sound?

You cared once. About stuff.
Items. People. Even music.
It's simply the background now.

You're not sad. Not really.
You just no longer feel anything at full volume.

Life seems to be on low brightness.
You seem to be fading,
yet nobody seems to notice
because you keep showing up.

Still posting.
A little too late, but still smiling.
Still saying, "I'm just exhausted."
(Once more.)

How much longer can you feel this way
before it becomes your identity?

Distractions

With the sharpness of growing silence in the chest like a
blade,
And sadness that doesn't let the heart rest,
I don't fight it with a cry or a scream of pain,
Instead I gather my thoughts, and search for a new
dream.

My mind feels like a lantern,
cutting the night with its light.
As it is burning with hunger
and glowing with warmth in sight.
So I pick up a new book,
and let the pages unfold,
Or dive deep into new music,
looking for stories untold.

I learn the names of stars,
or the names of the seas,
I try finding solace in foods,
 in different languages, or trees.
I let all this knowledge in,
in hopes to cover the cracks.
Because I learned that,
the heart stays safe, when the mind fights back.

I can't forget tho, cause, that wasn't the goal.
I carry it with me instead, with a gentler name.
Distracting myself is not running from it,
but healing with a step forward.
Walking on my own path, not trying to hide.

So now when the pain comes, cause it does so often,
I greet it with facts and information anew.
A better lesson, an improved skill, or a curious art—
Cause sometimes, the world helps mend what we
thought could not be repaired.

The First Yes

It wasn't loud.
No celebration, no drum beat.
Only a deep, drawn breath and a whisper
that she at last knew was her own.

She was standing at the edge,
where decisions were once made
while awaiting approval, applause, and others' nods.

However, only her eyes were important this time.
Only the one who understood the battle going on
beneath her skin. Was her reflection.

She didn't question.
Didn't resist.
Didn't fold.

She just said yes—
to the voice she had buried
beneath guilt and duty,
to the route that felt like the sky.

She recognised aspirations
that didn't fit into civil conversations

and mornings that went unclaimed.

She accepted the pain of becoming
and the excitement of making a mistake
and still getting back up.

Even though the world was full
with looks, silences, and questions—

She continued moving.

Because "yes" was acceptable.
Because it was hers.
Because she was the solution
for the first time.

Learning to Love

We called it love, yet I was still pulling back.
And measuring my value by how tightly you held on.

You made an effort. I know you tried.
To hold me through silences that weren't yours to
resolve,
and to carefully avoid the fault lines
that I never warned you about.

But I was a storm in a paper-walled house,
labelling every breeze as a danger
and waiting for the wind to blow.
I confused overthinking for care
and anxiety for instinct.

And since I hadn't figured how
to love the girl in the mirror yet,
I couldn't really let you love me.
The person who saw ends in every beginning,
who questioned the mirror,
and who made promises I didn't fully believe.

I did not know then, that love is an ocean
rather than a lifeboat.

And, I kept reaching out for rescue
rather than learning how to swim.

Thus, we sank.
And in addition to you,
I also grieved the version of myself
that I believed I needed to be
in order to deserve you.

However, in the silence that followed,
I slowly —rather than suddenly —met myself.
in decisions I made without regret,
And in mornings that I didn't dread.

I now understand that love isn't about being perfect,
or saving, or never worrying about failing.
It's about keeping the ground firm within yourself
so that your hands are open and not clinging
when someone reaches for you.

I am not quite there yet.
However, I'm close.
And when love does return,
I'll welcome it with calm rather than panic.

Reparenting the Sun

For a longest time,
I believed that I was the moon,
happy to shine in borrowed light,
satisfied in the silence of the night.
When nobody asked too many questions
and being alone seemed secure and familiar.

I discovered how to appreciate quiet
and trace the constellations
like questions I would never have dared to ask out loud.
I believed that being whole meant
being little, still, and sensitive;
I believed that healing meant hiding.

However, something changed—
not abruptly or rapidly.
The place where I used to dim started to get warmer.
A pulse that seemed like light remembering it was
always there,
simply waiting to be allowed back in.

I started talking to myself
as if I were important too.
Where none had been, I built delicate fences.

I quit referring to the hurt as "normal."
I quit referring to the quiet as "peace."

And in that silent work,
I encountered the light within myself—
slow, delicate, and fresh rather than wild and flaming.
A light to learn, not a fire to dread.

It wasn't aware
that I could have happiness during the day
and that I could be both -
the sun that awakens and the moon that observes.

So I could dance in the warmth
I provided for myself as well as in the shadows.

I get up now because I can, not because I should.
Since I am no longer only getting by in the dark.
I'm learning to appreciate the light I hold.
To be the sun and stay.

Things I am Allowed to Want

I am allowed to enjoy the sun—
not just its light, but its entire golden weight—
and to let it caress my shoulders
without feeling guilty about its brilliance.

I have the right to desire mornings
that flow as slow as honey,
filled with solitude, without any alarms or justifications.
Simply to take a breath and keep the window open to the
sky.

I'm free to desire softness—
the kind that embraces rather than erodes—
such as warm hands, velvety words,
and forgiveness that doesn't cost me.

It's acceptable for me to speak in colours,
to fill the room with resonant laughter,
and to keep my fire burning brightly.

I have the right to desire more than "just enough."
I don't need an excuse to ask for more love, happiness, or
time.

I'm free to desire books that make me better,
gowns that twirl, and coffee that lingers.

I am free to experience - hunger that does not conceal itself,
pleasure without evidence, and desire that does not apologise.

When I'm not holding the globe,
I'm free to want to be picked for who I am as well as what I offer.

I have the right to desire unearned sleep, illogical dreams,
and a life that bursts with colour, chaos, and melody.

I'm free to desire plenty—not as a luxury, but as an inherent right.

And I do now.

Too Big to Be Held

I can't recall,
The last time someone reached for me first,
not to give me something but just to hold.

They claimed that I was grown up now,
as though age were an armour,
and that I no longer cried in private
or trembled at my own image
because of the bills or busy mornings.

They dubbed it independence—
this silent forgetting,
this sudden calm where comfort had resided,
They no longer notice how heavy it feels when they look
at me;
they only see what I carry.

I move through rooms with the silent burden
of should-have-knowns and why-aren't-you-betters,
but the child inside of me clings to fear like a frayed
blanket,
terrified of disappointed eyes and doors that shut
abruptly.

I am no longer tucked in by anyone.
Nobody says, "It's okay to fall."
They see an adult, yet I still stumble
over the jagged edges of past guilt on the inside.

However, I'm learning.
I now meet her where she trembles,
kneeling with my hands open.
"You don't have to earn affection," I tell her.
Your own arms can handle the strain.

I rock her with patience and breath, not lullabies.
I transform into the voice that says,
"You are not a burden,"
and became the hug I rarely got.
I see her, even if no one else does.
And that's plenty to begin.

Centre Stage

She was never the voice, but always the echo.
The smile hidden behind someone else's louder
excitement,
the laugh a second late.
Every picture has a shadow with feet angled out
of the frame for precaution.

She discovered early on that silence might be safe
and that attention carried weight.
In order to avoid offending the light, she settled on the
edge of each room,
softening her footfall and editing herself down to the
smallest possible version.

And one day, in the silence between heartbeats,
she heard her name —not whispered. But called.

The sound was not one of shame.
But it sounded like a possibility.

So she got up.
With a steady, confident breath rather than a shout.
She moved ahead not to win approval or prove anything.
But to belong.

Now, the centre glows instead of burning.

And she stands there, imperfect and unfinished
but at last visible.
No longer serving as the supporting actor for someone
else's story.
She is the story's the plot twist, the rising action, and the
driving force.

She is the girl at the centre,
This time, she 's staying.

Inheritance of Hope

I once thought that the only things we carry on
are our names, customs, and quiet wounds cloaked in
tradition.

However, I've discovered that healing can also be an
offering.
A seed with kind hands and strong heart, tucked into the
future.

I have collected fragments of my history, not to bear the
burden of it.
in order to determine what should be put behind me
and what should be carried forward.

My silence will not be passed on to them.
They will grow up hearing love-filled yes/no
conversations and heartfelt laughter.

They will understand that kindness may start with you
and that being soft is not the same as being weak.

I will impart to them the lessons I discovered too late:
that we are allowed to blossom more than once,
that joy may be safe, and that rest is not something that

must always be earned.

They won't need to re-learn what I've already left behind.
Rather than beginning where I hurt,
They would start where I healed.

Perhaps it is the purest form of inheritance—
not the suffering that moulded me, but the hope I chose
instead.

Becoming

I know what is right, now.
What makes me feel like myself,
what makes me happy,
and what gives me peace.

I've felt it, experienced it, and chosen it—
but, not because someone said I should.

I talk clearly, not loudly, but with my entire voice.
I no longer measure my pace against anyone else's;
instead, I go about my day in my own cadence.

Knowing that I can be whole without permission
The realisation that I don't require approval
to be whole makes me feel more at ease.

There is no need to please or prove anything;
there is only the silent power of being me.

I adorn my days with items that provide a warm feeling.
With individuals who see me just as I am,
with words I believe in, and with the colours I adore.

I'm already her, growing from the inside out.

This is the feeling of becoming:
a constant blooming that is grounded,
genuine, and bursting with light,
rather than just a beginning or an end.

www.ingramcontent.com/pod-product-compliance
Lightning Source LLC
LaVergne TN
LVHW050945200726
843508LV00011B/2451